Test, Orange

Test, Orange

Cherry Smyth

for Kate,
with best wishes,
Cherry Smyth
11:11:12

Pindrop Press

Published 2012 by
P_indrop Press
Mallards
Steers Place
Hadlow
TN11 0HA

www.pindroppress.com

ISBN 978-0-9567822-7-4

A catalogue record for this book is available from the British Library.

Typeset by Pindrop Press.

Printed and bound in the UK by the MPG Books Group, Bodmin and King's Lynn

Cover: Nicola Tyson 'Running Figure', 2008, oil on canvas, 76 x 60 inches/193 x 152.4 cm. The Artist courtesy of Sadie Coles HQ, London.

Thanks to the Arts Council England.

For my parents, Ron and Ailna

Acknowledgements

'Transparency' was commended in the National Poetry Competition, 2010; 'From Trouville, 1865' won 3rd prize in the Torbay Open Poetry Competition, 2010; 'Return to the Figure' was runner-up in the Gregory O'Donoghue Competition, 2010; 'Wishbone' was commended in the Writers Inc. Writers-of-the-Year-Competition, 2008 and published in *The Long Poem Magazine*, 2009; 'These Parts' won 2nd prize in The London Writers' Competition, 2007.

My thanks to Judy Brown, Uriel Orlow, Mikhail Karikis, Nina Rapi, Oreet Ashery, Patricia Clark, Mimi Khalvati and members of the Advanced Poetry Workshop, and Angela Gardner.

Much gratitude to Chateau de Lavigny and the Tyrone Guthrie Centre where some of these poems were written; and to Hugh and Noreen Clark, Jane Pillinger, Charmian and Paul Buckley, Marianne Klopp and Laura Hatton, Jennifer Russell and Godfrey Offord, Kirsty Robinson and Jonathan Hall, and Simon Marriott for offering their homes as London escapes.

Thank you to the editors of the following magazines and websites where many of these poems first appeared: *Poetry Ireland Review, Succour, Magma, Staple, Cyphers, Chroma, South Bank Poetry, THE SHOp, The Stony Thursday Book, nth position, eyewear, foam:e, White Collar, Famous Reporter, Domestic Cherry, The Moth* and *The Stinging Fly*. And to Joan McBreen, editor of *The Watchful Heart: 24 Contemporary Irish Poets*, Salmon Press, 2009.

I am indebted to Farley Mowat's *People of the Deer*, Michael Joseph Ltd, London, 1952 for the poem 'Caribou' and to Patricia Dienstfrey's *A Woman Without Experiences*, Kelsey Street Press, 1995 for 'Wishbone'.

Other books by Cherry Smyth:

One Wanted Thing, Lagan Press, 2006
The Future of Something Delicate, a pamphlet, Smith/Doorstop, 2005
When the Lights Go Up, Lagan Press, 2001

As editor: *A Strong Voice in a Small Space: Writings From Women on the Inside*, Cherry Picking Press, 2002, Winner of the Raymond Williams Community Publishing Prize, 2003

Contents

Transparency

In Japan, in a laboratory in the hills, a man is whispering to water.
A man, whose wife has left him, is focusing on structure through
a powerful microscope. He's astounded when each isolated drop
seems to listen, absorb the words, change like a face transformed
by smiling or a splash of shock. He studies how words like 'family'
or 'betrayal' alter the crystalline mandala, as if the vibration
of his heart shakes and resets each miniscule aquatic form.

He mouths 'eternity' in Arabic and 'goodbye' in French and manages
to photograph the crystal as it clouds inside like a blown fuse. Now
others will believe him, will apply the knowledge he's not built for,
why these lexigrams appear, as if water held the capacity of mind
and how minds change when love's ear hears nothing anymore:
how different from the first unspoken, this last not speaking.

He's tired. He doesn't mean to murmur 'mercy'. It's almost a
forgotten word. The droplet he is viewing becomes a spiky lattice
with a strange core, like the trapped blue-white sea of a cataract.
His vision softens. He asks mercy for himself, from himself, until
the mantra rises to a song from the southern shore his wife would sing,
a song of waves and Bo trees, whose words he's no idea he knew,
and he sees the water tremble as if for the body that once carried it.
'Forgive me,' he says. He photographs the feeling.

Tarantella

She will not move. *Black.* She will not eat. *Wolf.*
She will not speak. *Spider.* Yellow incisions through
the shutters do not vary her. She is a piety too far.
Call for the musicians. It is Puglia, 1691.
She is the land's disobedient smile. A painting bitten
by a man. She is the goods. Rush the eddy of drums
at each ear, swim her in sound, play until she begins
to flicker, rise, to spin out the poisoned circle of herself,
the handsome horseman, dance; unwind the coarse wool
of her cliff mind, her winter sea, dance; (*to think she mistook
the sea for kindness*); dance, out of his leather reins,
faster, until there are no currents in her, no flow of 'I';
giddy as water on hot oil, the shimmy of faces into her cure;
(*rage before the plea for love*); dance, spiralling a trance from
floor to ceiling, clears her head of bareback colour, rakes
her soul from its sacrum. She's basted in the crushing sun,
shriven by the drumskin's batter – stinking, famished, skinless.
The tare and tret are taken down. Bats come to tie up her braids.
Seven nights of fit have forced her this side of something
that will do. Will take the hand. The thread. The family lace.
They kneel to praise Saint Paul, slaughter a young goat.

Loch Na Fuilla

1

On the climb to the loch
we got lost
spoke to a man
– why do you want to go there? –
who wouldn't advise a swim:
the lake got its name
from three children drowning

we expected death
to glint like a blue
eye of sky
a level metal
but coming into sight
it hung to the crater
in a brown sere bowl
that looked contaminated
but by what? Rust, bad rain, or –

closer it appeared to quiver
in vertical streams of fawn
as if the loch was in process
waiving itself
a lacuna of pins
where water should be

a heron rose
a single, always single bird
not the grey flower of bones
it would have been
if I'd been alone

there was no swimming
no traversing the tight valley
of reeds and sedge
closing by itself
like an eye with sleep

here was death
its own haven
the settling was a rising up
a scrim of tussore moths
a levitation of tulle

2

The difference between a bog and a loch is time.
The space between a death and a name is myth.

3

One foot slid in first
then your leg
it was already happening
when I made the mud
the hole it was becoming
real
an active suck
pulling you under
'Sinking sand' my mind told the dream
as your face sank in
then I thought I'd be the stronger
the earth's hunger versus mine
the primordial, then me –
ha!
You were gone before I thought
of how I could save you
It involved a sheet roped under your armpits
and a big haul

4

Tibetan Buddhists say that how you deal with nightmares
shows how you will deal with death. The swamp dream
vanished until I read the word 'swale' in a poem.

5

There was no drowning
my father said
only a story
to keep the children from going there.

Glen Haiku

Pushing a granite hunk
from Feely's quarry
I come back to my desk

Wild wet on the deck table
can't erase the rings
from summer glasses

Ash branch sunlit
from a splitting cloud –
her smile at the car window

In the glass brown river
Lackagh Bridge
draws its stone-washed oval

Overnight on the gravel
around the house
springs a garden of snow

The blizzard left
a grandchild's green bucket
a pot of snow, no footprints

Forgive me, Robin,
I said you weren't red –
in snow, you rouge

America in Colour

(after Russell Lee's photograph *Jack Whinnery, homesteader, and his family, Pie Town, New Mexico,* 1940)

1940 – before America got fat, got camera-ready.
Everyone does as they're asked.
Watch the birdie!
Except me,
the one in the pink frock dotted with four
black buttons from Nana's Sunday coat,
some precious, broken trinket in my hands.

The man from the FSA wanted us inside,
planted like a pew of pinto beans
against the wall, lined in brown paper,
night edging round the curtains –
Papa in the centre, muscled and earnest as a tree stump,
Baby on his lap, next to Mama, shying like a mare,
too overworked to look straight anymore,
one twin on her knee, the other at her shoulder,
and Boy, arms folded over best braces, like he knew
he'd conquer any world, eyes alive with revenge as a rat's.

I'm gazing up, mouth slack, wishing
I'd another face or shape, trying to look
anyplace but into that city man's dark snout,
where magazine girls smile, raise bottles of Coke.
The flash bursts its silver balloon,
leaving a scrap of white cloud
in the sky of my eyes.

From Trouville, 1865

The season is quite over and everyone has left. The bathing huts
are shut, the beach pleases itself. Jim, obsessed with news of Chile,
wants to sail to Valparaiso. His eyes catch on the horizon. There is
no-one in his paintings now. I've seen his back. I was his sea.

Gustave looks less at the misted rocks and more at my neck, my wrists.
Yesterday his finger counted each pearl button of my blouse. He asks
if he may brush my hair. Some won't touch this red; some it hurts
because they love it so. I move like a flame between two draughts.

Trouville has none of the sadness of London's autumn. No coalsmoke
bitter at the throat. The clouds are fast and full and bring a change of light
that never is the end. The chill is always gentler when you can
be out in it. All evening there is talk of hue, of stroke, Jim fighting

against too much reality, Gustave arguing to keep the visual truth.
He finds Jim's pieces all too bare, 'sketchy'. Can't he see their breath-
less plenty, their search for foothold is just as real? The girl in white
has gone. That fresh sensation. I am more weary of the pinch-faced

mother than I am of him. He made me on copper, drowsy, half
on another plane. I am no ghost. Why isn't the living world enough?
I'd spread out my hair so it could dry. Dropped flowers were my idea.
They did not last the night. How we laughed on that bearskin rug,

fur sticking to our limbs. I was seventeen. I knew that love had kissed
me, exactly where. That poor girl I was not. Stay still, Jo. Hold it!
I'll move now if you please. I lost a promise once. Now I play
at promising. The idiots cannot see the drama in the tones, the flints,

the threads of white. Her prize, his cage. The old Academy duffers
have rebuffed him once again. The dying rooms for every trophy girl
or blandest babba. The lost lily of her eyes. Millais saw it. Blankness
this side of disappointment sinking in. The rest went frantic. We're off

to the Salon des Refusés. Next, I will take supper naked on the lawn,
Jim will lounge in his kimono to be in better company. I stand for
months in that cambric dress, fingers winter blue, listening to day arrive
and leave Pigalle, Jim hopping on his long legs – hand on hip, busy

with cigarette or brush, those dancing eyes that feel every colour
of my skin as heat and cold runs through me, the way some feel
certain notes. That sneaky, sinful smile that each time gets me going.
He takes me more alive than anyone. And if we're sweet and sad,

I'll sing or act a scene from strangers met at Wapping. I'm in such fine
form, I whistle! Jim bought me a grand black bear muff and
an enormous bonnet. He loves to watch how they gawp on St Germain.
Then love's work in curtained light, when I must be deeply still,

breathe when he breathes, a kind of mouth-to-mouth with eyes,
the look-of-life, I call it, when I see far back into him, my brightness,
to America, to Russia, and he sees through me, the passing glow
we know will pass and I make it art and that has me in heaven.

Caribou

I have beaten the lining of the coloured sky – Kazimir Malevich

To stay still is to die. They have no home. Their only history
is the five hundred miles to go. To see them is to see boulders
roll out of white, a slow brown foreground in achromatic time.

They eat on the move – dwarf willow leaves, lichens, sphagnum moss –
scraping the vast plate, chain-stitching through the starched Barrens,
north of northwest, where no one is thought to live.

The doe come first, heavy, urgent, as if magnetized,
but no compass can hold this north so close, a fatigue
to sweeten all insomnia at the coldest end of air.

Unsullied by the trafficked heap, they swim in white,
above the gessoed bright green undersea, the folds of tonal shift,
as soured milk lifts its tinge of glassy blue.

The bucks follow in an undulating mass, manky, fallen kings
who once gave approval to mankind to raise their cone tents
of hide, wear suits of fur, feed off a muted, bow-slung kill.

Then the joy of fleshing space
where blinding lead-white tastes
like the whiff of tarnished silver.

How it moves the heart, the wrapped stillness,
the flash of world in newborn eyes, the eye-white's
target of your seen beginning.

They cross the forest of white snags, the skull point
of no arrival. New circles draw them in illimitable
space, the air bred with stinging smoke they must outrun.

And only some can take so much abstraction
before snow turns their eyes inside out, like larvae burst through skin
and discard the host on beds of white on white.

Once moving in a mighty sweep, fewer now twist
a line, piloted in squalls of wire through the tundra's
blast, where ice flows thinly, its beauty incomplete.

Reading the Cup

In the cup of fresh verbena leaves
Michal says she can see the sea at Cuas Pier,
the floating, sun-filtered green we dived into.
To me it's the Chivers jelly shade the green blinds
cast in summer afternoons in Portstewart Primary,
swimming the room in broken rivulets of light,
anointing us with sleepy calm, as if this degree
of blurred daylight was hallowed and our behaviour
had to correspond, like visitors to the continent
who mightn't be allowed back if we didn't show respect.

I remember glancing up from my jotter, the trail of wet
ink, like a seal above the sealed swell, to breathe from
the focused hush, before being drawn back down into
its one complete body, and the open-necked indulgence
of Mr Morrison, who would rather have been up the strand
on such a glorious day, getting his lamb-head tanned.

The rare heat, the gentle knock of the blinds against
the windowsill, subdued us in a soft erotic stupor,
like being here, dazzled by the sea, glittering in inlets,
warming on the rocks, hazy with clean air, tongues of sea mist,
the absence of man-made sound. So I stay at my desk,
hot sun sprinkling through a cotton gauze, thinking
of what Louise Bourgeois said – art is made of all
the things you desire that you say no to.

According to Patti Smith

I tugged at a dead rose branch.
It snagged and snapped a healthy one.
I left them to their mess of thorns,
the spread of wither, a dried winter's red.

A friend carried in a crown of violet,
performed with scissors and vases about the room.
I breathed the squeeze of women's kisses,
the expensive mist of a small woven lung.

'When my husband left,' she began,
'he shook me free of explanation.
I fell from summit's air. Then where he saw
merely hurt, I saw his beauty. Everywhere.'

I'd never seen the faces of this coin,
but I could see she kept it in her eyes.
The shine of knowing from unknowing,
the freak ransom in what had come to war.

When Patti Smith lost her husband,
then her dearest brother, pain's crack
almost broke her until she sensed
their best selves recur through her.

She said that on seeing *Guernica,* Jackson
Pollock took the drips, just the drips
from the horse's mouth, flung them out – the blood,
the tears – stood rampant in the joyful scatter.

Relief

Beside the painting of nine trapeze artists, with its indigo
corner of coloured stars, tall, grey platforms and rows of letters,
was the same painting in relief for fingertips to read. Not being
blind, I hesitated to close my eyes and feel. The memory of the
black silhouettes was cold, those flying bodies no longer flew –
the air around them, quite spacious to the eye, was solid wood
and the hard grey structures felt unsafe for landing. My touch lost
interest among the lino letters that refused to spell, like some last
typesetter's debris. Instead of this neat, crafted equivalency,
I wished for a physical experiment that forgot sight, took
the body up in a carousel, harnessed and secure, and swung it
around the gallery to notes of flute or organ. Then everyone
could sense all along their floating, circling limbs
the acrobatic discipline of paint, hear the urgency of unreal stars,
smell the singed, disjointed letters and taste this twilight, driven
world, the awkward, fallen splash of accidental gold.

After the painting *Did Germany Put the Sun There?*, Thomas Brezing,
2007, at the Crawford Gallery

Playing Guitar

I'm thinking of first flesh, exactly when the creamy
swelling above the stocking rim, the impossibly
old-skinned balls gaping through a pair of shorts,
took on taboo – that luxury of sight, the accidental
invitation to an adult world I smelt all around but
hadn't yet reached to touch.
Then sitting one sudden summer afternoon
with Elaine and her stepson on a garden bench,
taking my T-shirt off, letting him enjoy my black
lacy bra, knowing I was on a line she kept drawing
in her head and I kept stroking like a guitar string,
not plucked, but slid on, making an awkward sound
sex the air, the grass, the trees, making the boy's bare
eyes swivel and swivel away again as if he hadn't heard,
with Elaine carrying on the conversation,
nipping the deadheads off the marigolds.

Rushes

(for Jacqui Duckworth)

1

That you could handle film was like touching God. That you could lift a spool in your white cotton fingers from its can, from the tower of cans, and thread it onto the Steenbeck, was like showing how God moves. I watched you in the dark make thousands of tiny decisions of light.

2

From spool to empty spool, the images clattered, a baggy ribbon of blurred flickers that you paused, lifting the hood and lining the strip with china marker. You pulled the film out of the gate towards you like two elastic arms and settled it on the metal cutting block. You spliced and taped and fed the scene back, a minute shorter. You numbered the end, fastened it to a bull-clip and hung it on a hook on the wall, or slid it into a suspended cloth bag for trims. Then you clicked down the hood and made the movie move again.

3

We'd flirted at a feminist film group. I'd noticed your walk – a loping swagger on long legs in tight jeans. The static between us made me giggle so much I had to leave the room. You didn't want a relationship. I made you have one.

You'd sit at the edge of your seat. You couldn't hear anything else when you were editing. The images were sound that needed an exact rhythm, a melody only you could detect. You knew to cut just before it seemed to need it, your attention surgical. Thelma Schoonmaker sat at your right shoulder. When we watched *La Regle du Jeu*, I didn't flinch as the dozen rabbits and birds were shot. You'd taught me to go inside the cuts – 102 in 4 minutes – counting Renoir's rhythm, defined by Marguerite Houlet, his editor and lover at the time.

4

We met in unadorned rooms in Soho, in basements, or at the end of a grey corridor where daylight never arrived. The sun burnt a bar of gold on the ceiling or the wall where the blackout curtain didn't quite close. In these dark and smoky places, you showed me what made you, making sense of every film I'd ever liked, teaching me why, giving my passion a possible world. We never had sex there. You were paying by the hour.

5

Film buffs were men. With beards and BO. We were cinema fiends. There were no videos or DVDs. There was the ceremony of cinema. A von Trotta Double Bill at the Academy; a Bergman Triple at the Electric; midnight cults at the Scala; Monday nights at the Everyman. We travelled, stayed awake, skived off work because there were films to be seen. I'd smuggle in a bowl of finely chopped, dressed salad, fresh bagels and two forks, and we'd sit silently nourishing ourselves for hours. You never stood up until the last credit, as if by reading each name, honouring each member of the crew, you could absorb their skill, their magic.

6

You were in love with many women. You appreciated them like a connoisseur of fine liquors with a longing roll of the eyes and a small gasp: Gina Rowlands in *Woman Under the Influence*, Bernadette Lafont in *La Fiancé du Pirate*, Giulietta Masina in *Nights of Cabiria*, Sophia Loren and Catherine Deneuve in anything. You were a big flirt and a big fan and I didn't realise then how much humility and forgiveness that required.

You forgave Deneuve her bad plots and her love affairs with ugly, much older men; you forgave me my younger women. You were capable of devotion. You knew the difference a 25th of a second could make to a glance across a crowded bar.

7

You were a celluloid master. I bowed at your feet. Once you rescued a bored porn star from another bad movie, devising a way she could cut herself free from the film strip and escape on the back of your motorbike. No one believed it would work. Or the 16mm feature you made of the threesome you were living in, in a flat in Warren Street in the early 80s. You ate only toast and tepid tea. But women always fed you more.

8

You gave me a Super 8 to take to Russia, showed me how to use it. I carried it like a baby. I shot blossoms falling in a Moscow park, a gigantic mural on the dull outskirts, a sudden heap of tomatoes for sale on the roadside. I couldn't film people. The camera was a gun I couldn't point. I couldn't see a whole from parts, came home with short unfinished poems. I don't know where that footage is. In a grey can somewhere, held closed with white tape with my name on it, on a dusty shelf in some cutting room.

It Takes a Worried Man

Dad understands the beauty of miles clocked
up along the corridors, no more roads
for him, the one who taught the ten to two
of the wheel, the three-point turn,
the one who wants to meet a wall at speed.

They wish he would rest, see what settles
like shapes only lain snow reveals
but motoring his body, eyes dipped under
the feathery confusion is the only way
to steer the vast drifts of reason's traction.

My cap at an angle meant to cheer
– *Take that off. They'll think you're weird.*
Where have you gone, my dapper, dandy one
who drove singing that he'd not be worried long?

His mouth trusts anything I offer
but this fierce homeopathy – anxiety
for the anxious – isn't curing – the white room
painted to look yellowy green, all exits locked
and filmed – *will I ever get out of here?*

They say the drugs' diversion will take weeks.
Should I believe them or smuggle him out,
a sack of Foyle mussels over my shoulder,
let him get lost in his own way, a fiction
walking down to the cliff in his dressing gown,
when my back is turned, his point as lucid
as the lighthouse that identifies the pier.

I leave like an accomplice in an ugly greying sleet,
a winter more unknown than any other.
He's left with no good coat, soft shoes,
head bare – a last leaf on a lawn.

All night I've asked should I, could I
return to hold down a pillow over his fallen face
and if the answer lies in our pact to always
do our utmost, in any dicey situation,
to help halt the other's pain.

Fairy Tale

She knows what she is doing.
  The guardsmen are soft with solstice,
    careless with so much darkness.
She bathes in goat's milk to be kid-tender,
  asks her lady-hand to comb her hair
    as if it matters.
She's told she's beautiful, some kind of princess
  and tonight she believes it.
    Her eyes glint scimitars.
She listens for the owl call,
  the pop of carp breaking the surface.
    Her bed is made ready.
She drifts into its down, quiet as a snow hearse,
  flattens her palms on the linen, as she should,
    enjoys its handiwork for the first time.
She has four seconds while the lady-hand
  turns, four seconds for one hundred years
    if it's true.
She glides the hidden needle
  from her laced cuff, pierces her finger hard,
    sees the red pool spread
a map of deepest sleep
  over which she flies
    and watches herself flying, futuristic,
      untouchable as an entire world,
        dancing on the head of a pin.

The Back of My Hand

Will the ashes that rise up meet the ashes that fall – GC Waldrep

The rain this summer rains so hard, it falls up.
Plosives of rain. Tiny detonations of smack.
Your face if I saw it. The other end of a kiss.

If love is a kind of rising up, how much slower
this falling down. I dismantle the warmth with
hands of ice, parcelling it up for a different keeps.

No two people share the same cellar. It will not
be raining in your eyes. You'll nurse your soft-toy
chemicals, your severe and urgent needs.

But I know where your desire has been,
you felt-lined thunderhead, you weather exile!
No mirrored windows are repeated twice.

New conclusions wait in sock-soled series
to lick the back of my hand. They will not answer
to error. There will be sun. It won't frighten us.

Stone

Your thumb almost covers it,
moves back and forth on a vague hollow
as if this was truth,
as smooth as skin, but cold.

It is as thin as a pound coin
minted by the sea
for some sort of exchange.
The thumb spends where the eye can't.

It is the static mouth of a sand body
that was washed away.
You can't afford to remember it.
Everything between us ends with a stone.

Windblown

I'm watching rain run mauve into silvergreen, wondering
what reading shape you're in and where your enciphered
pencil tracks have led. Was it wrong to think you'd only leave
in death, or stupid, even though I always said you'd vanish?
How come I came to love believing that, like staying
on the TGV headed in the wrong direction?

What we intuit from the start doesn't seem to bother love.
Love watched me reach you a bowl of Spanish olives
just beyond your grasp, saw like a stranger how passivity
weighted you for things to happen. Love didn't mind
the little blindnesses that hid my self, those you never hid,
mimicking my version of what together meant, close as an espalier.

Once, in a noisy flat in Venice, I looked until you stared.
'What are you doing?' 'Trying to see in,' I said. You told me
that you could not reveal me further – 'What if you died,
left me hanging?' The practiced, pitiless set of your mouth
showed the path was closed, my body lay across it.
I could not lead you there with any perfume.

We took a boat, lay on white sand under parasols, claimed
a patch for the wordless. We made the end the centre and ate
around it, touching it less, its fierce, consuming heart, turning
pages in the dark. You saw me in my best ten minutes before dusk.
I watch the clouds let the rain go. Sunlight hits my wall
with noon enthusiasm. I cannot make it stay.

My Intended Past

Memory re-enters from its separate life
enjoying that hot afternoon in Barcelona
or the walk in Ards Forest last January.

The trick is to slip into the fold
that's there in its own present: tell yourself
they're just a couple, in a corner

of looking, sometimes smiling, often
silent, and they're growing smaller,
dimmer, making their way without

you to cool off in the air-conditioned
gallery, roll, hot-footed in the inflatable
bubble tent; see them come through

the ancient Scots Pines, identifying bark;
see one always be the one to reach
for the other's hand as they emerge

onto the empty, white beach, you crouched
in the low dunes, watching the couple,
unremembering what they're saying,

the easy, soft speaking of inattention,
the dailiness of trust and triumph,
complete, open and expanding,

while you turn away, follow the blue
arrow-trail back to the rental car, reversing
out of the spot, out of all the gazes you ever

shared, back to the strong handshake, the first
hello, the setting eyes, before the gaze came back,
your future overgrown in its stare.

December Morning, 2007

The lake is running from the wind
caught in an inland tide,
the mountain's opposite.
We cannot walk on it
to get distance, gauge its fill.

Sunlight is playing
a small gold fiddle
in the branches of a tree.
Belinda may not last till Christmas.

Dying is always happening,
holding up its dark mountain
from the depths of a lake,
questioning the summer table
on the winter deck, the unplanted earth.

On the beach, the wind is carving
tiny pinnacles of shell.
Look what the sun is doing
to this miniature world.

It Hurts Less to Be Hurt's Teacher

To grow out of something
not need to do it anymore
not need to make events

happen so that she could
peel off the back of her voice
prise open the gloat

standing in the harmless sun
plucked to joy
by the cry

her rush to rescue
the little one from the dark shed
delayed

or outside the bedroom door
after the sleepy story
the promised panic from the pitch black

a bulb between her thighs
till the wail delivered the most wanted –
the acute body – arms like pliers

the hyacinth wintered in the school cupboard
the too-white shame
of its water-frail roots

the sorry song of his words:
this hurts me more than it hurts you

later her dreamt theatre of small children
siblings even
who deserved something

for standing in a row in white underwear
against the bath
unresisting as cotton

in fear that adult eyes on beaches
could detect which side of the door she was on
watching the children play

Still Life at 44

In your office, one afternoon, you pointed
across the yard to an empty house, windows
boarded up inside, one bay window open at the top.
A grey blear hunched behind the pane.
'It's birds,' you said. 'They fly in and can't get out.'
Then the shapes became distinct, the pile
of pressed feathers, furred hats without heads.
I imagined their efforts, flapping below flight,
                                        beating, beaten back.
'I've been over there,' you said,
'flung stones to try and break the glass.'

Months later, I watched them move
your arms, stretch your legs, change
the feed in your nose. Your eyes flew
round the room after the trapped words.
I reached for your hand,
                          waited for the shatter.

The Ethiopian Church in Jerusalem

We stepped barefoot into a pink gloom, lined with painted
staffs, as if shepherds had passed and time quieted back
from cars and fumes, the calls of Arab workmen and Hassidim.
A hive of music rose from the chambered shrine.
Through the curtain, a few ancient priests whose mellow drone
was dying out as it was sung. I travelled the bassline to Tibet.
Where did you go? An indie concert in a faster city? Or some noteful
place you're orphaned from and this tourist duty a reminder?

There was war going on. I tried to make it mine.
We watched TV between languages, the frantic home-made
gurneys, the lofted corpses in Hamas green, and amid
the weeping, chanting, the azan's failure to withstand the bombers' sky,
the heaped discrepancies no help could penetrate.
Your timid homing roamed alone; I wished I could've stood
on the other side of any border. My dreams accused me. Never you.
I knew war's private weight only in the wake of ceasefire.

Were there golden stars on a blue-domed ceiling?
Those roped off partitions, underlit, I thought I could enter,
before a finger hushed me out. Then the yellow jasmine afternoon,
the pilgrimed pavements of Jaffa Road. Lintels overgrown with figs,
homes ramshackle with extensions or desuetude, the unenhanced city
outstripped your melancholy and my response to ritual.
You had no church in you. I had too many.
Each of us too well-mannered to be outraged enough.

That night neither of us slept. Tanks advanced from that ground.
How could we sleep? The stars were Gaza's stars.
I read you a guidebook history of anti-Semitism
in a long and saddening prayer. We pushed our single, hostel
mattresses together on that level floor, that seemed to detach
and float south as if to achieve a rescue. By morning you'd hoarded
all the flagrant hurt. The flutter I thought was birdwing
in the flame tree was the tatty plastic of a white sack.

Marching on a street at midnight

in a comfortable city while war
is eating away at people, homes,
schools, the new year comes
scented in a bottle of arak
held out in a stranger's hand.

You'd think we could have smelt
death on the wind from the south,
seen it blacken the horizon,
bloody the sea. Parties bubble
over pavements, people drinking
into no tomorrow, some yelling,
'You homo scum!'

We march, chant down the avenue,
pause for the boy on crutches.
Your kiss searches mine for faith
in what we keep faithlessly doing.

Yesterday, hate high in the papers,
haters surrounding us, on a ruler road
made by tanks, I told you marching
changes nothing. 'Nor does poetry,'
you said, 'or music, yet somehow
we do it, involved in useless
making until it's a need met.'
How I loved you for that.

Now, across this cusp, we hold up
the tragedy our voices will not grow
used to, move slowly in a body
towards thinking some kind of act,
larger than killing.

Hanukkah Candles

It was a small trodden thing on the street.

The street wasn't even a street.

The face was unseen but you knew it was there.

On a crushed street of still standing angles.

Someone cried from a tower in the prayer of a tree.

The tree had dropped its fruit before time.

Prayer had wiped out the street, ridden on the small face.

After the Cast Lead Operation, the 22-day Israeli offensive in Gaza, 2008-2009 in which at least 1400 Palestinians died, 400 of whom were children, and 5000 were injured. Thirteen Israelis died.

Schooling

Tipsy and bold in the first skirt of summer, I cycled
past the Almeida where a knot of boys tied up the road,
a white one hitting a black one with the leg of a chair, a ring
of white boys watching, two women sipping wine
at an outside table, pretending it was a play.

I asked if they were just messing about. 'Yeah,' one said.
The black boy hobbled up and stayed. I almost left.
'Don't be so nosey, man,' said another. That classroom putdown
of my curious child flipped it. 'Can't you see I'm not a man?'
Jeers netted me. 'Why you got short hair, then?' shouted the first,
his fringe in a girlish flick. 'At least I'm not ginger,' I said.
I said that. The other boys laughed. The one with the gelled
and beautiful red hair did not. He let out a puff
of shocked air, stooped to pick up a stone.

I began to pedal, felt the fast wind of the throw.
I tried to look sedate, cruelty seeping out behind me.
Dusk through the plane trees in Gibson Square greened
the houses, cramped the streets, like a tank I once saw
in an ancient aquarium, packed with as much rock as fish.
Five huge moray, tapered like blades at each end, coiled
their dull tapestry, tapes of muscles swimming over and under
each other, like pairs of hands trying to wash themselves clean,
then lying too still, gulping at the water as if to speak
of the hunt, of colour, of distances. 'They feel nothing,
know nothing, you know,' I heard someone say.

Using the Bathroom

The room with no windows
overlooking the sea,
tiled with exquisite blue and green mosaics
like boiled sweets that shone if licked;
the room with a hot press, ironed linen, powder smell;
the room with a vent the cries went through,
with a thick wooden door that shut us in;
where it happened, the room at the centre of the house,
where he could be dark,
where he wasn't thinking,
at the bottom of a mine,
what it would look like,
where he bent us over
the edge of the bath
good leverage, bare,
where we'd plot to shit right in his face
or withhold sound, victory,
numb as enamel,
no begging or weeping
before his hand came down.

The Food of Secret Wonder

Up on the mountain above the treeline,
nothing grows in the grey talus of chipped earth
that slides unsteadily as breaking ice under
the paws of the she-bear and her two cubs.
She brings them there for secret food,
under the rocks, live cutworm moths, pressed
like dull flowers, the colour of dusk.
She claws off the surfaces to light, instructs
her cubs to forage in this summit desert
before the snows. They scoop up thousands
of the wafer nutrients, must find freight-loads
of moths to sustain the coming winter, each wing
a delicacy, each skeleton a fat-rich crisp.
The mountain was made for the moths, the moths
were made for the bears and the bears were made
for the wildlife camera crew who ask how to get
some colour into the scene, until at last a male bear
comes courting and the female must fight him off.
They swipe and tumble down the slope in a brown
bulk. Somehow the mother wins.
Wounded, she climbs the jagged scarp. Her
scavenging paw is bleeding. Close-up red.
There will be no more feeding. No more filming.
And the moths, camouflaged and cool,
resting in diapause, will be lifted by nightfall
like living dust, be blown to alight on almost
imperceptible, transparent flowers to drink.

First Days in the Caha Mountains

What does this stillness do to the body?
Incremental expansion like chocolate weight.

The green puts its mouth down to the water.
Thin drifts come to blue the high lake's window.

Eyes stretch to a twenty-mile grey harmony.
Sky shifts like music, the self following.

Luxurious air creams out to meet space.

Edges made alert to movement and noise
ease up to drink the silence but don't yet.

Distant intentions wander into purple.

Wishbone

All things are tragic when a mother watches – Frank O'Hara

Not An Ordinary Afternoon

It is not an ordinary afternoon.
It is the third day.
The mother says she feels useless.
The daughter carries her to be useful.

They try to write, to draw pictures together
but the kitchen table rears up between them.
– *There's so much needs doing.*
– *Nothing needs to be done.*

They lean ironing boards into the wind,
grate skin into cheese, into lemon zest.
There is never a mention of blood.
It was an opening no-one noticed.

No Meat

The not enough shifts and shivers in the living,
tight under the arms as last summer's dress.
There is no illness here. They pull it in on strings
from outside to make common sympathy.
The daughter's subdued by soft furnishings.
There's no meat on people she never knew.

The mother ruffles recipes, glazed as a pear,
looking for the woman who entertained dozens
from a galley of cookery books at the touch
of a dimmer switch, the flick of an oven glove.
She doesn't stare at the sea, but glances measure
the offshore weather, rain banding the headland.

The daughter's eyes roll out to the horizon
where a tanker has dropped anchor.
And underneath the impeccably lined curtains,
a sharp word waits. One of them – the b. –
will use it for the warmth in friction that lets them
soar together for a moment, then blow apart.

Then they'll crave again, salt the aubergine,
dab the bitter juices, brush with oil and grill.
They'll eat, tentative as tasters for a queen,
mannerly, the *mmm* coequal.

*

Pick it clean and let the bone dry.
The two of you break it in two.
The one with the larger part gets a wish.

Crop

The daughter writes a film script to know the next scene.
People are leaving her cinema. There's not enough action.
The mother claps, believes the future's in television
and full make-up.
The daughter learns that what she knows about her place,
where she is expected, she must have known as a child.
She has spidered the knowledge in her bones, her posture,
the way she enters a room. She looks for the beautiful to unlock
it in herself. To dare answer it. The risk is often too great:
to make a mark, make a blank surface useless.

The daughter makes a pot of tea. Ordinary tea.
Warm the pot; a teaspoon per person
and one for the pot.

Let it draw.

She can see what she is producing.

Only here do verbs catch in her craw,
the self she's made of sugar and sticky-up hair
dissolving on the living room floor.
She wants to speak of the time she counted to nine,
christening, unchristening, imagining the blood
not going to waste, swimming in a cold dark lake.

*

They have become as cotton to wool
from one root, one cell, schist and silk,
showing love in ways each didn't count:
the olives on the branch too salty
for the one who craves sweet,
the leaves on the branch too sullen
for the one who needs gloss.

A Doing Word

'Every day's an action day with your mother,' the father said.
But he can't use the washing machine, the iron,
prepare a meal for six, tend to the sick, remember a birthday.

A mother is someone who goes over the edge
but comes back briefly to set out glasses of milk,
bread and butter for her children.

A mother is someone life takes a hand out of.

A mother does shit.

*

They sit in court.
The mother is top judge,
the cruellest outfitter.
The daughter is lowest clerk,
the unreliable witness,
What is it you do exactly?
To doss is to lie about and do nothing, says top judge.
The jury of dining room chairs
rock on their back legs.

*

Sometimes the mother forgets who she's talking to,
starts talking from a past she rarely visits.
The daughter sits up. White sparks scatter
making an arc leap between two metals, welding a join.

*

Does something have to break for a wish to be granted?
Is legacy in the bone set free when it's broken?

Bring on Water

The daughter is a not a mother. She is a big mouth.
        Things go in there that shouldn't.
Whole libraries. Weekday mornings in bed.
        They both forget, start up words, engines on different fuels,
burning at the same rate, hungry for the same race,
        to be seen, get applause.
The rally-driving mother drives the hoover through furniture,
        into corners, up walls, pulls off her crash helmet,
shakes free her long black hair.
    An alarm is ringing.
All the daughter wants from the smoking house
        are the mother's sketches, her watercolours, laid between
tissue paper, in a plastic bag.
        One is the wall, the other the ground, one terrified
to leap, the other frightened to receive, both knowing
        they survived the jump, the weight before.

*

There is tundra at the window.
The daughter has snowboots and skis.
She can dart like a night beetle on water
pulling a flash of moonlight,
a rucksack of scripts on her back.
Who will buy? Who will buy?
All over the land, women are asking.
So much to sell if only it were made,
if only it were shown.
Things they made up:
a line, a stroke, a tap of work.
The daughter throws a lifebelt to the mother.
It is made of concrete.
There is only breath for one.

Ladylike

On the fourth day, the daughter looks at photographs.
Time makes the mother shy.
Hair black, skin white, eyes silver blue.
At the Taj Mahal, the pyramids, in Gandhi's house,
a balcony overlooking the Aegean.
More Irish than she is in Ireland.
Was your mother a model? they'd ask by the swimming pool.
She would sit in an aura of hairspray,
knees bent to her skirt, her femininity
done in a rush, always pulled off –
Murano glass that walked.

The daughter takes a close-up,
no hair, no clothes, no context to get under,
to get the mother she thinks she has.
She hasn't time to smile. Her eyes steady, unsurprised.
Her cheeks relaxed.
The daughter says thank you,
tells her she is beautiful.

*

The mother remembers paintbrushes in her pockets.
The pockets of a pinafore she wore when she was 12.
She left them on the island. With her wooden palette
and the mantra 'I will be someone.'
She looks out from her home, clean
as an urchin's test, eaten by wolf eels
and sea otters, bleached white,
pores where the spines used to be,
Aristotle's lantern gone in the tide.

Shadow Bird

When she's rowed all night,
the daughter watches the mother
sleeping upright in a chair,
crossword aproning her lap.

Her light white hands
fluttered a shadow bird
on the bedroom wall,
her thumbs its head,
knuckles the furcula.
They can hear it in the silence
they cannot keep.

Now it's soft battle. To spin
on the spot until you're so fast
you're not moving. Wind
a cocoon that unwinds
itself constantly.
It's harder to make than unmake,
softer to be than to do.
Half hard, half soft, loving,
they look at each other.
Three down, the mother asks,
a way through. Seven letters.
They make hot toddies,
crack cloves in their teeth.

When a Mother Watches

I see my father and my mother in her.
His daydreams, her busyness.
Daddy's girl with parts all right for a man.
When she came she was
everything I ever stood for.
A love plum I wanted to eat.
Such happy hunger I tried to hide it.
I lined up all the things I wanted to teach her
so she'd learn quicker, hurt less.
She acted like she already knew.
She was me and more. The more shot up,
spat out, stung my eyes.
She wanted the world more than me.
I hadn't meant for that.
She puts me in a chair, probes with a steel tool.
I don't understand the need for dentistry.
She wants the only thing I kept to myself.
I've hidden it in the last place she'll think to look.
Whatever time of year she goes,
it feels like autumn.

Transparent

Today something might happen.
They play chess with draught pieces.
The daughter scoops the bobbing teabag
                    to the draining board.
If there could be ceremony without bother,
with grace and from the centre of both of them.
Both suspend their lives' strangeness
with this stranger to take tea with,
neither knowing how to place a true word,
a meaning between them,
each thinking, *poor scared darling,*
postponing looking over the cliff
that they'll come to, if they're lucky,
each in a selfhood, certain, dear to each other,
see-through, visible.

Do I make myself clear?

The mother is the well and the water.
The daughter is the bucket and the rope.
The mother watches the coin of light go dark and light again.
The daughter moves up and down never quite reaching the surface.
Come a little closer, they call to each other in the cool, dim shaft.
The mother wants to see the horizon.
The daughter wants to slake her thirst.

*

What do you do when you are the wish
the gift was given up for?

Fresh Air

They strip off in the patio of sudden sun,
unbend in jointed chairs, high-factored,
their faces shielded with some thin thing,
talk drifting up the rockery of bold hostas,
escallonia and montbretia bowing
green swords to the ground. Lazy for once,
allowed to lull, they examine bits of skin,
glimpse how the other's body is doing.
Turned to the sun, they could be on a cruise,
by a lotus pool in a mountain villa, leased from
each other's view, the weight like a bowling
bowl that rolls on past where it seems bound
to halt, lighter and lighter on the green.

On the Last Day

The daughter plunges
out of the Atlantic, caped in cold.
The mother has drawn her a deep bath
like she used to when she was a girl.
Getting in, her skin is so spent, it cannot tell
if it is hot or cold, has shed its heat in the sea.
She rolls her flushed body in the shock of the gift.

The daughter looks at the mother.
Considers how she could work
from the outside in, birth in reverse,
to deliver the hot rush that is her own.
To furnish her like light
going back into a candle flame,
filling it with what it is full of.
If only she knew, if only they could
translate each other into what's valued.
Not a table, but the wood it's made of.
Not a page, but the reason you'd turn it.
Not a destination but how slowly you travel there.

*

Once, the mother gave the daughter a wishbone.
The daughter thought it was a tuning fork.

After Goodbye

The mother will only draw for a child
as some women only write for children.
        The way the mother draws,
the daughter could watch for hours.
Her light white hand coming in to land.
The mystery of the line, before it joins up
with another, its purposeful poise, and then
the way she continues the movement of the pen
after the mark is made, as though her mind
is so involved in conjuring, it forgets to stop
and keeps the hand drawing for a second in the air,
like brushing long hair when the gesture lasts into space,
the hair lifting after it, electric, attached.
        Knowing where to end the mark, the daughter
thinks, takes such confidence, and that small uplift
of the hand is the most eloquent, graceful thing
she has ever seen – the fluidity belongs to her,
becomes an extension of her veins, a beautiful
pulse the daughter does not have.
        She realises watching her mother draw
that she was made instead of the drawings
and the paintings from her mother's pulse
and she feels the sadness of her mother's leaving off,
finishing her, her head tilting to one side
to see her work, appraise it, the daughter
        left aware of space.

Back to Back

This cinema that needs
no darkness
spooling bloom

overnight overfed pink
heads bunch
and brag on branches

perfume loose
and bareback
rides in from the gardens

back to back
petals zoom from buds
mouthing May

colour red, colour yellow
color Techni
disregarding fences

Your Lover

You were kissing me hard because I was alive
and the woman you loved was dead.
It was the last time and I knew it.

Your lips had narrowed and the sun
hadn't reached inside the creases at your eyes.

Tears sprang out of you. It was my job to bring you back,
like after an accident when you can't drive again.

I had my own purpose: to go through you without catching fire.

It didn't even hurt, like a page being written on
in a book full of writing done for years, years before.

I held then I let go, turned the wheel into it,
as if on black ice. Later in Sainsbury's

when I floated down the dairy aisle, elbows
and knees not following, I recognised the sex
we had, the hours it would take to douse myself.

Lifeguard

I swim, she walks
the length of the blue.
I catch her eye,
make it a bubble under my hand.

I tumble-turn in her sights,
push away walls.
I send wet sun up
to spray on her mirror.

She sits, owl-faced,
her glance promiscuous.
Her body is sober,
ticking over.

If my splash becomes thrash,
she'll dash-dive in,
shore me in fish arms
and swallow my mouth.

Looked At

It's in the eyes. The eyes of men shorter and wirier than you
that can see straight to your pussy, have been there in dreams
you had no part in – the Spanish one in the Irish supermarket,
the Irish one in the English university, the African-American
stranger in a New York City park who said he could tell the feel
of the hairs on your thighs, that he liked women to be unshaven.
'Try Germany,' I said, but I wasn't cross, because I could see
into his balls, where our babies lay, all hirsute and milky brown,
growing quiet and visible as a kink that's waiting for its
moment, ready to leap like a struck match in the right eyes.

The Only Way Out

From the house on the hill is a mountain,
strung in narrow feints of black teeth.

Salt wind rears up the organ pipes
corrugating the slope into wet air sounds.

Roads hide in hedges – only the telephone
poles figure a way out – or the waveless sea.

Beyond the shoulder crouches a cupped lake,
its walls tilted like the last view from a plane.

I spend my days planning what to dig up to eat.
Sometimes a sliver of yellow is chased overland.

In a field at the back, grease-fingered boys
scramble wrecks in a wreathe of dust and fumes.

Drum and bass blurt out its suffering over the gorse,
the heather, the hills, to city clubs along the wires.

My eye finds the butterfly roof of a 60s bungalow
and keeps returning to its flowerless line.

The only way out is to stay in, harden,
strip to the studied harmony of windowed skull.

Inland

I didn't mean to but I kept going to where land was moved
every day by tipper trucks and bulldozers, in a turmoil of dust.

Tracks threw up broken tiles, old toilet bowls, rubble from building
at the coast, that had thought it could lie dormant.

Pathways appeared overnight, hills of banked, used-up cement,
as impermanent as the balconies and rooms it once furbished.

Away from the long lanes through olive groves, the slopes traced
with Roman ruins, the Moorish village clutching the hill, I walked

under the flyover, a faint talc on my skin, because the light at the dump
recalled a white beach – formless yet coherent, shadeless, changing –

I didn't know what it could give. I witnessed the last
patch between the playa and the pueblo because it needed that,

and I needed on my tongue the ash taste of Spain,
eating itself up and spitting it out again.

DO NOT SWIM NEAR ROCKS

(for my father at 80)

'Do not swim near rocks' is painted
in red block letters on the white wall
of the steps, yet kids still love to jump
off ledges of basalt into the crescent pools
the tide carves as it tries to be land, where
the current cords through the fabric of water,
tightening to a navel beyond the horizon.

Dad, whistler, lover of jazz, of wine,
of seafood, kept a resuscitator beside
the garage door, a mask, a pump, a rubber
hose, that came from the other side of
drowning and could suck you back if you
so much as looked into its black dome.

Someone did, running into difficulties
tragedy can never fully describe.

Dad saw them pull him out, a great
big handsome lad, winter-white,
begin mouth-to-mouth. He ran for
the pump. The waves crashed on,
everyone suddenly cold in the sun.
My father looked up.
    Said how he expected the sea to stop.
        The roar, the rhythm did not.

And I wonder if he hadn't fetched
that contraption, would his own mouth
have been the thing to save him, his heart's
insistence pounding up a choke of water,
his lips filled with life's wilder sustenance
and his blood running in time with the sea?

Lost Bees

I

I am the plane tree
looking out, tall and full,
as if nothing is wrong.
I reply to the wind,
let in August light,
drop a scrap of bark
that has filtered air
to the pale yellow trunk.

I am the oyster in the lagoon,
working a skin of pearl
over some grit, to smooth it
into a part of me,
a shell embryo
I will have to let go.

All around are waters
where the thin crusts
of sea creatures
fail to calcify
and fish move north
collecting history in each scale,
cooler, growing less,
winter a dark ring.

I am the sky,
clear as a fine china
of blue air, bone and fire.
You'd think I would ring
and not shatter if tapped
by a hammer from space.
All across me, chiasmic
streams of burnt fuel etch
a design some find pretty,
like acid on an intaglio.
And below, riots for food
have already begun.

II

We walk well protected into the sun.
We hesitate next to a wheatfield
where pesticide hangs cloudless.
Yellow flowers are ranged in the long
polytunnels of a fast summer, watered
on timer, and beyond lie empty frames,
plastic shredding into a brutal fallow,
annulling distance and provenance,
like a jet that never lands, a plenty
that will not ripen.

III

Eyes shut, we feel ahead through
wavering thickets of light, branches,
unstrung pearls, the passing shadow
of a plane, to feel the first fear
and stay in it, for every surface to come
from somewhere deeply renewed,
and the delight in finding it there.
We're preparing to erase our traces
to zero. Starting with what we have seen.

Safe

Black stripe, white stripe on the lichen-green
body of the tit – do birds still fly over Fukushima?
Its industry reassures, two miles from our power plant,
its busy beak, into leaf, out of leaf, healthy.

Waves on Japan's east coast break a swash
of ceasium-134 and will do for thirty years. Will
tuna grow multiple eyes to peer through the spoiling?

By the river, we miscount the peals of the medieval
bell, believe it's earlier than it is. Iodine-131 travels
on easterlies – we admire things that can pass
through walls, the invention of half-lives.
The mole knows nowhere dark or distant enough.

A tectonic spasm takes seconds to shake out deep
cities, break open what earth can't nurture, neutralize.
Still we herald the spent rod, as if it's all we have left.

Today we are downwind, we breathe more shallowly.
The breeze is no balm, the rain without merit.
We press washed wool to our faces.

They say the river is toxic – downstream.
Downstream – they say the water self-cleanses.
Downwind – smiles of development; jaundiced,
bald quarry on the riverbanks, feeling the cold
of this hottest unknown.

Above the birch forest – how we love our cloaks of invisibility! –
stacks pump vapours into our future, and we whisper:

> Forgive our atomic litter,
> our living with impasse,
> our no, but yes,
> angling for safety.

Six Given Fields

What will you do when it's your turn in the field with the god? – Louise Gluck

Lust

When he rushed me off the road to the field,
I forgot clothes, food, all kindness, lies
grew out of me, cover-ups, alibis.
We tore through the crops, insensate to harm,
terrorised by scent, flat-out in mudsheets;
limbs of leaves, glazed, we bent down the cob
to enter us better. We furrowed each other
with the vision of Futurists, desecrated
chapels, blown-off family; taut with return
to our random start, where cells clarify,
float in a cry and the soft-boned body splits
into memory, giving birth to first form,
all the white walls of time collapsing,
left interspatial on a serac of this.

Love

'Forget the field,' he said. 'Empty your pockets,
throw away everything with your name on it.'
My heart ran faster after colour and taste.
'See that wall,' he said. I did. It was beautiful.
A painting on water, it moved and stayed still.
It reflected me as I'd never appeared.
He taught me to worship it, then he said,
'Go up and stand with your face against it.'
I did. The nearer I got, the longer I stood,
the duller it grew. I flamed and dropped.
Dust, peeling skin, stains of human and dog.
I wept for our wall – that's what he was after –
said, in tears, we are strongest, purest matter.
I licked my cheeks, purchased binoculars.

Art

He whistled Telemann below my veranda,
waved a flag of hay to spend in the wind,
drew how rain fell among camels of straw,
dreamt a caravanserai to vanquish my airspace.
Crouching like nudes in a closet-free circus,
we wrestled the light into bone and sepulchre,
made Vorticist love in trains across country,
singing Brecht from windows of Yves Klein blue.
He slowed down the speed and thickness of sight
till holes in the head were slashes in canvas
and the glad of the glade rivered thirty-nine greens.
I was arable in his white, framing hand.
Those scorched by too much of the real would pass
their burning air by the field to be cooled.

Patriarchy

He holds my elbow still, trying to usher me
up the aisles of his fields. He grips my wrist
when I speak with too much vigour at dinner.
He thinks I've done nothing, been no-one.
He's surrounded by statues, can't be budged.
If only I'd take his name, keep to home
and heels. He has names for women like me,
uses them in the bar then in my face.
He paid me to take care of his children
so he could fuck me at the end of his garden.
I followed the red of his cigarette,
wore his wife's dress. First it smelt of sugar
being baked, then it blackened to smoke. My hair
never grew back. I hide it. He prefers that.

Money

In that field I rarely had to turn up.
I was video-phoned in my court-shoe neckline,
my quirkless beads, as I unfolded my desk,
lit up my terminal and my fingers bled
so I could be human, life expectancy
whizzed in a file to the Head of Risk,
who used two replies – OK or stop!
I ate my lips in alien buffets, fell
under his table of mortality, slipped in
trips to Hong Kong in over-chaired meetings.
He rode his limo, I took the dawn train
among a world of fish I'd never known.
I emerged with a wallet full of new teeth,
powder traces of avarice under my nails.

Age

When he called from the field I pretended I couldn't hear,
straightened up, widened my eyes,
ignored his Prosecco, his dark walnut liqueur.
He read me Jack Gilbert, Wislawa Szymborska,
said why not go down to the Rhône, swim in its water,
so milk green you'd think it was ice-melted glass.
He led me into the purple vibration
cicadas make in the dark, said hear as one
the rush of the river, the rustle of leaves,
lie down in the stubble and be entered by sky.
He sat still with me till I knew that this body
is it – is not it – is all – is nothing,
that the field will change its colour and texture
and we'll see clear to Mont Blanc once the leaves fall.

Land Art

Nike rag and bone and knee flint
have dragged cabinets, sideboards
in a perverse removals to mark
an identity seen from the moon.

Scaffolded towers with no insides,
the cross-sections of a boundary
built in heads in 1921, laid in
concrete closures across border roads.

Boys shimmy up these mountainous
isosceles, clad in tyres, topped with
the Pope, but can't see beyond Cave Hill,
couldn't care that hands calloused

with a rare labour will pour
with water blisters tomorrow,
for they'll turn skies, Brit the night,
lodge their thunderhead of smoke

make air sick with it, rally ready eyes,
sculpted in the fight of flames, white
cloth handshakes, drum-rolls, Harp,
a struggle-straggle fiefdom

after loyalty passed on –
these grand, guarded keeps
gone back to waste ground,
a hole in the sky, a rolled-up flag.

Montjuic

Everywhere we go, we come upon the remnant,
the name a living thread – Jew Street.

Between one city and the other, we forget to load
our suitcase, experience a brush with fleeing

in the multi-story car park – the precious choosing,
folding, foolish, your face wiped of colour.

I tell you that all we need is a toothbrush, that
running water makes everything renewable,

clothes will dry in a flash. We'll check in bare-handed,
giddy, proclaim our idiocy romantic.

Still, in the shuttered room, you check your backpack
again for one of your three passports, then say

you have to lie down, loosen the grip of what's gone
missing. And I, so briefly dispossessed,

touch what I stand up in, aware this fabric
that connects, protects me, could curl and desiccate

like singed hair at the turn of circumstance
or in the extremity of some belief.

Cold Burn

Mist was breaking above the sea
like its own warm breath into bitter air
or the steam from curative springs.
The sky's blue confused you, a tepid sun.
You ran late, after the crowd
of Christmas bodies, out of the throng
of whoops, whiter than sand,
strides extravagant and pressing,
then nimble at the wall of waves
as paper near a flame.

After bobbing, screaming, you streamed out,
sticky with salt and snot, turning blue,
veins sea-tapped, aghast
with frozen ecstasy.
All day you were so fully in yourself,
burning up doubt faster than anyone else,
your kiss marine. Later that look
returned from early photographs
of bewilderment that you'd come
out in time before you died.

Happy Slapping

(for David Morley, murdered at the South Bank, 2004)

Walking at first. In a group.
Loose energy like too much aftershave.
An embankment. A bridge.
She laughs. He gets her on his mobile.
Space makes their bodies snappy,
fingers beat-beating like a kid for Ritalin.
They flick insults at smaller selves, bump,
kidding up the steps, chase over the bridge,
running above the oily stir, invincible as air.
Below, two guys to their five, sitting
watching the river churn the lights.

They don't need the time they ask for.
One clocks a punch. Simple as.
He goes down sweet, makes a ball for feet,
a kick, a laugh, caught on the screen.
Strikers, they score forty, giving it all,
not given in the listening rows, not asked for,
till they're cooked in the triumph of making
blood rip through time, opening up the night sky
to their bigness, their matter, for nothing,
their own visceral news so new it sends
spears of sound and picture up to satellites.

Written During Teaching in a University

(after Adrienne Rich)

I want bear. The thrusting head,
with a hardwood brow,
a body that can rise
into a mountain. I need bear.

I need claws to dig up what's buried,
tear open what's whole and
a roar to fell trees.

Give me bear blood in a bear cape,
a baggy shag of a brute to show you.
Bear that can lift bulk and run
as astonishing wind.

I want the long seeing of its small eyes,
the love it makes with shadow,
the inconspicuous night of bear.

To call it. Bear. To bellow it. Bear.
Make brick crumble.
To reach into bear history, pull out its cub,
spin in a bear dance with no watchers.

Father-in-Law

He cannot look openly at her body.
It is too woman
and she is my man.

He asks her questions he answers
about histories
so-called for a long reason.

That she is a Jew is in his skin
like a tick
he can't feel apart.

He goads in the third person
while she is reading,
his favourite pastime.

They'll never see their best,
their only open,
their only on my one to one.

Enough

(for Lloyd Haft)

I was in a very dark place then,
the poet said, as he handed
me the volume and I can tell
from the lines that he thought,
this is it, how to get used to it.

London is getting ready for leaf,
for night, like us moving
in the lit-up bus for warmth
beneath a dented moon.

Cranes guard Waterloo Bridge
where a woman swings a banana skin
by the stalk, seen through the smudge
of grease from a rested head. The man
beside me eyes my red leather shoes
and white ankles – no tights.

I am not coming home from work,
I am coming home from reading.
You can hum and think at the same time.
You can be in the city's belly
and sit in deep silence.

I pass out of the bus behind
my neighbour and could call to him
but the city has not healed me enough.
He walks ahead in a grey suit,
fingers already playing the piano,
as if counting up his secret joys.
I'm singing, *'Yellow River,*
Yellow River, you're in my mind,
you're the place I love',
and am half-way through the chorus
before I realise it.

Crazy Paving

I lead him to the park up the sunny side,
make him sit, close his eyes, hear breath.
I talk quietly into a spell of emptiness,
show the hem of my guide in a wave,
a muddy glass of water settling. 'Yes,'
he says, 'yes,' as if the trees are a church.
He has a plane to catch, peeks at his watch.
I hold his hand, bring him back to the bench.

'It's funny,' he says, 'where
Nana and Papa saw God, you see
the sea, moments in this world.'

Then I'm aware of a seam of bright moss
outlining the crazy paving at our feet,
as lead keeps stained glass in place.
I know that if he'd been well, we'd
have missed this softly-packed exchange,
its crooked lineage of looking inwards,
the mysterious requirements of pausing
and discipline he thought he could skip.

Inheriting the Books

(after Eiléan Ní Chuilleanáin)

They slink over at night
rustling their paper jackets,
some damp from the swim,
others sipping Bicardi and Coke
and giving off the smell of cigars.
'Mine eyes are laden with salt,' says one.

There's no room on the shelves
so they stack up on the carpet
trying to see out the window,
catch a glimpse of Big Ben,
the Houses of Parliament
or the rooftops of Ronnie Scott's.

At night the big bruisers flap
their foxed flyleaves,
start pointless debates
with the feminists, the poets,
their Chicago accents
whining under the door.

They have a nose for blood,
for six-shooters and broads
who'll let you drive when you're tight.
They've been asked to keep it down,
to lay their hands face up,
but a voice always comes back –

'Ask not for whom the bell tolls.'
We shut up.

A Clean Echo

Yellow butterfly, too fast to follow, stitches
primroses to air in Latin, Greek and Hebrew:
Héloïse waits on pins behind the gated walls.

Blossoms tremble in alerted breeze as the sound
of a horseman brings his letter south and lifts
the demeanour of the abbey stone.

'No man will touch you if I cannot,' he writes,
'like an enemy who destroys what he cannot
carry off.' Such frankness made her comply.

Abélard's letters strengthen then enfeeble her;
she cleaves to their honey, their axe cleaves her;
she must close her casement to the evening linden.

How happy his hands, his mouth, in the glisten
of her perfume! Dark robes place her now among
the common, as if shame had not burned her through.

*

Nineteen when Abélard schooled her, whispered
that her looks, her eyes, her discourse pierced him,
and she kissed him where he was most wounded.

Lightly as a bee he landed, stung his *nominatissima,*
led her to her own mind's shining threshold,
that toiled to temper her body's quick surrender.

They shepherded their secret love, believed their bodies
lasting temples until white petals loosened from the plum,
counting two moons without a sign of blood.

She could not conceal a crying babe, told him she could
cherish freedom as his mistress, but he pressed her
to become his wife. At first light, they slipped away.

Soft, open, peaceful, their marriage bed,
but darkness delivered her uncle's men to geld
her husband, a punishment to make flowers bleat.

*

Pewter days, the cool nave, the quietening rain of prayer
touches her in Aube woodland, touches him
in Brittany, out of the world and into God: their pact.

Grass pleads with the wind to let it be, early
peonies fall, frayed by hail; the shadow of the swallow
cries for what is lost higher in the sky.

Her leaden steps seem to push the cloister ground
behind her as her figure marks a standstill; at night
the moonlight lays its window tomb along her.

Héloïse cannot forget how her cheeks hurt with laughter
– squeezed muscles' joy – her thoughts lamplit in his,
how her heart lifted her breasts towards his embrace,

how each rib held the imprint of his grasp, when lungs
expanded their curved cage, as if he were her air.
She'd inhaled willingly what most there never would.

'If that were a crime,' she writes, ''tis a crime I am yet
fond of. The man was the thing I least valued in you.
Comfort me! Nothing is ugly when you are by.'

*

Her poems to God arc to Abélard; how to counsel
him to better rest or tilt his longing heavenward,
how the fine launch of spider thread, now brightness,

now invisible in the wind and sun, was a golden silk
spun between them, renewed by nature daily. She fasts,
studies, weeps for piety to quell her.

Love hangs in a hush around her, enclosing, chosen;
others pray a lifetime for such an aura: a trust in the best
in all that lives, that drives life's sweetness.

'At the other side of great desire rests great devotion,'
his letter says. 'Being divine is our continual closeness.
Let's walk the cinder path of night's hot hearth.'

A fisherman once told her that if caught within a dervish
whirlpool, twirl under, into it, and it will let you go,
as though drowning had a lid only the courageous

could open. The currents confuse her. The tall trick of it.
Her hands raise up as she goes down. Palms open, she asks,
can I hold to this abandon and yet still be saved?

'Protect me walls,' she prays, 'as bark protects a tree;
spare me, mantle of earth, from the sap that rises
and resounds like music from your fevered core.'

In dreams her tears hang like icicles from her face.
She sits each winter long, so frozen, no thing can warm her,
learning to be empty and still flesh.

*

'It's all for nought,' he writes. 'The fire is only covered
with deceitful ashes. 'Tis a thousand times more easy
to renounce the world than love. Héloïse, I am not cured.'

Stringent sickness, silence, steady her, her quill her sword.
'Here love is shocked and modesty deprives me of words.
What a lame master who cannot not yet master himself.

'Hasten less to add more fire. As you yourself taught,
"to fuel" means "to cling to" in an Eastern tongue.
Your words tighten around me as flames that steal my air.'

She has said what mattered, what made matter to one man –
how could she utter her heart to another? So light he made
those heavy words. Meaning spoken once from the rock;

knowledge touched once in the river; their wisdom
theirs alone: a clean echo. The bells told hours
but not the years it took for her to know

their love existed only in understanding and also
only for the understanding. Love made them children,
joined, running; grief made them parents, separated,

searching; devotion made them gradually,
finally, one orbit circling in history
and in art, each with steepled hands.

Centuries later, the lovesick, lonely through
some great injustice, re-enshrined their coupled dust
– one bone button, one carved buckle.

Return to the Figure

When most of my father's friends had died, he began
to build columns of round flat stones. He stood them
by the front door, the windows, as if to harness
companions for the thresholds. They watched the sun pass
with him from the Limavady mountain, over Mussendun,
to the lip of the headlands of Donegal. They were never
spoken to or named, but drew the eye like something
that doesn't need, yet composes living form, the way one
thing supports another – the head, the neck, the torso –
or lets it lie along it, like one rested hand resting on another's.
Dad wouldn't call himself a sculptor, but this is art, just as
the Inuit traveller once built stone men at each new bend
of water, upsurge of ground, to extend their home's
periphery, the touch they'd left behind, so forward steps
are always manned by glancing back. Later travellers
discovering these sentinels felt held in the plural's
heated hands, believed they could cross the void unharmed.

These Parts

It was a howl to start myth, like Demeter without her
daughter, up along the track lined with orange groves.

To walk into it was to walk into the way life is,
the two girls, fists in their mouths, shoulders peaked,
eyes unlearning a secret. It was a fattened, hairy sow
held across a wooden table by seven men. It was hard

to see what they were doing – bleeding or skinning it alive –
some surgery the mountains had a taste for, hands busy
with it, stroking, touching – their words a quiet, loving hymn.
The thyme and the rosemary grew on. To step in
would have been to convulse scenery, speak in gravel.

The track rose into the hills. The woman I was walked on it.
Her throat was closed, her ears seared with death's bellow,
the men's patter. Only then did she reach up to a tree,
steal her first orange.

Pressure Front

Today cloud has reached the garden, is trying to bury
the house, suck back the sea. I bring coins and go
out into it, to cut free the rain with my scissors.

If I drive, there's a sparrow in my ear
from Dublin, where it's all sunny, and covers
of covers I once danced to with smoky hair.

I don't follow signposts. I loop, park
at a gate and walk an unmarked road
up vanishing, bedraggled rockland.

The farmhouses have insistent lawns.
A collie sickles towards me, full-uddered cows
stare. I think every limestone crag my size

or taller is sacred, a portal I can stumble through.
Grass sprouts a parting in the gravel,
leads me round a corner where the lane

ahead is spanned by a peacock
in full bright radius, moving like a big hooped
petticoat almost taken by the breeze,

its emerald eye-ends swaying on stilts of quill,
its pert throat a jewel, psychadelic blue
in the falling moss-grey damp;

its lust so built, bursting the line and gravity
of the place, it comes on like an attack –
the shimmer that rises after rain.

To Dursey

We were crossing to the island in Ireland's only cable car,
a patched-up crate, its windows malted with salt and spume,

the floor cracked with straw. We held on, knees locked as it jolted
over the steel cords, then steadied in a heavy catch
Dursey was reeling in.

I prayed my mind be light, my body airy, worried about loosening
the door should we plummet, when you signalled to an open pane
to look down to the pale sea

where the moving shadow of ourselves seemed to attract spokes
of sunlight to its square hub. It wasn't the headlands,
the ruined church,

the long unsown furrows, or the waveburst on the rocks below
we'd come to see,
but this green star, its vehicle flimsy, worn, but its energy enough

to wring the ocean's clarity into a show of underwater, thistled light,
as if the water reflected what air cannot:

the pull of perception itself, making us sense that we could cast
into the essence of anything and shine through in another world.

Other People's Money

Saturday's were good in the counting room,
thumbed piles of a hundred, bound in a rubber
band, a sacrilege of biro on the top note;
the serious smell of coppers and leather,
ledgers transfiguring the departments below
into totals. I saw my father's exacting formality
in an aura of warm, slightly nervous, respect.
I counted so much of it, other people's money,
between 16 and 18, exposed to its quiet,
concentrating fever, I gained an immunity.

Later, my father, long retired, sits me
and my mother at the kitchen table, presents
his money files, his dockets, his policy numbers
and tries to transfer their knowledge to us. We
nod vigorously, ask questions that reveal how little
we've understood, like a telephone pole trying
to talk to a leaf. He becomes skittish, shouting,
and in time, the three of us are in tears. Not
because there isn't enough, but because Dad won't
believe, and Mum and I can't get the decimal
points in line. We're stuck in this balance sheet,
desperate to make out our own bodies, somehow
put them together again.

We coax him back to things we can handle, things
he's provided, the cup, the saucer, the plastic tumbler.
And all around him we can sense the years he can't
be sure of, how many, how much, and the not
knowing has jangled him loose. My mother
and I know nothing, have never known. 'We'll manage,
you know,' we say. We've always managed.

10 Items After Diagnosis

I

Three rings of pain
the ring of ear
the ring of jaw
the ring of skull
each with their own
unsayable consonance.

II

Into the machine
the hook up to cure
is the norm
destroy to heal
is against all
I have taken to mean

III

is life.
And the lover sobbed
just to imagine what
will happen to our human city
this love cluster
of Peppe, Luciano and I.

IV

How long? How dense?
How fast? How come?
Jesus, I believe
in the light channels
where faith doth
open in white.

V

The C word sucked
never swallowed
last thing, night,
first thing, morning,
its black flavour
everywhere I look.

VI

We climb a hill
an ordinary pavement
in dusk, three healthy hounds
hungry for painted spaces, colour lines.
'One in three,' I say.
'Which one?' says the sky.

VII

His bed is empty but for him
I could lie on the other side
but he snores, gigantically.
Sleep looks for
the fifth side to lie on
if there was one.

VIII

Milk is said
to be
not good
anymore
Is it time for miracles?
I ask you.

IX

I don't know how
to begin with I
as I is second now
after you
in a queue all the way
to the distant lights.

X

I count six beams of X.
Each day for six weeks.
One for balance. One for understanding.
One for your soul. One for your upper limit.
One for the place it began.
And one for luck.

A Bottle of Mineral Water

When a green light pushing sun through February
hit her page, she called it moods, talked about hair,
a heatwave, thought it was the thin sticky leaves
of the Chinese gooseberry, taller than us, amazed it grew,
throwing a moving stain. She always looks for the hue
of light, edges framing a metal door jamb.
There's no colour to radiotherapy. It carries energy
so fast it shrivels what it meets, knows how,
like this sunlight, to make a green figure shone
through the hard glass of a bottle of mineral water,
a leaf of light, falling. Giacometti sacrificed
the whole person to work on the head, till drawing
a glass on the table in front of him was all he wanted.
'The more I take away,' he said, 'the fatter it becomes.'

Now You're a Woman

Here's a space I can't stop being in,
a shape given by body, by mind,
a form that controls what isn't,
that is good to know.
No man knows this.

*

The limbs that forgot themselves
were child's limbs,
abandoned, goofy, barely gendered,
hanging upside down, look at me,
rolling tra-la-la on the grass,
in the soft, wide daisy of the body
that likes to press against earth.

*

I was so intensely girl
I thought I'd never look adult
at the mystery of children. And I do.
As if steam remembers being water,
water misses itself when it is ice.
They say memory evaporates
in three dimensions at least.

*

Nine years old and I'm in love with my bike,
talk pony to the handlebars,
not guessing I've something to prove,
something to protect on the saddle.
I'm all elbows,
jumpy with life,
aware of none of its uses.
My brother gets a bike with a bar.
This is the beginning of not.
The meaning of skirt,
the boy-girl ratio on the plate.

*

She came in shyly, an odd clearing
        in her throat, full of feeling as if
                holding a gift I couldn't see.
She placed the word 'cushion' next to 'blood'
        and 'baby', a soft upholstery,
                but there was a shriek no-one heard –
that I could split like that and seal
        was beyond speakable.
                Like, 'will it have a scab?'

To walk around with this sinkhole
        that would wound at any minute,
                was my first stupefaction.
To be told something so inner, a subdivision
                I never saw coming, was the second.
                        For two years I yanked at my pants
to witness the dark daub. Time enough
            for fear to take on her pride.

*

So, if condensation collects, drips back
purer to its source, I'll sweat it out,
be girl again – no ruddy clock.
Let the corpus luteum close its niches.

*

I hold the stain on my fingers away
        as if it didn't belong.
                                I licked it once
so I could know everything,
        searching out names for the hole
                        a stone leaves in a plum,
the curious Q-tip.

I want only air at my thighs.
        The sacrum slipped off-kilter
                as I crave to be supine

or sat on a stook of grass, apart
from everyone.
My belly's a melon,
breasts transparent with hurting,
nozzled to the tap till bursting.
And from the centre of my brain
an iron horn grows,
knocking into things,
a stumbling unicorn, ravenous
for fucking at this fine
edge of self, where loathing distils;
then the labia glisten, parting like
sleep with a puff,
and behind me I drag the blotched
bedding of my own little abattoir.

*

bloedsed – bleeding – blessing

*

My calf pulses like a hard young breast,
muscles squeezed into lips,
hands sweeter with myself.
I train for hours before beauty.
I am elastic, juice of pineapples in my veins.
I marvel at the tones of her.
She is flourish,
an exclamation mark,
drawing air and water, till hot, harsh splendour
collects me in her thoughts,
is carried away with mimosas on the 8th of March.

Such a miracle to find food for all of it,
mouth feeding, brain fed,
touched yahoo
and it's free, painless and multiple –
the longed for supple romance,

                    the twirling baton of neon.
Mouth-watered serene,
a silk sound,
a dazzle falling for real this time.
          The music is inside, gorgeously yes.
          She touches like night on day.
          I gain it all without fists.
She holds me under, in, through, to the brim of us.
Equilibrium of fire on water,
          shimmering elegance on the surface,
                    fanning out, bodies ringing like bells.

*

– What shape are you?
– A bidet of felt.

– Where do you sit?
– On the throne of the cervix,
  hands folded over my fundus.

– Are you happy?
– 400 times or more I've prepared myself,
  lain down the red carpet. What do you think?
  No one comes to my wicker gate.

– What do you know?
– A little poetry and a lot of complaining.
  I'm packing up. This place is getting me nowhere.

  I'm going to wing it.

*

My daughter was dreamt as a monkey on my back,
          light as a rucksack,
          coming with me everywhere,
                    as books poured in and out of me,

lovers knelt to love.
I gadded about, busting with belief.
Every joint pulled to the moon.

Yesterday the words 'my children'
hung
in the drying curve
of an oxbow lake.

*

That's it. Now, I'll be male, more in the world,
less watching the small growing things
other people need, less spit on a tissue.

*

Not that I didn't weep
in a public toilet in San Francisco
touched by the stark string of red cells on the bowl,
the tadpole of non-life,
shed like the reason I was called girl, woman.
All roads lead to mother.

*

I am a quick-moving river
no time for time's
interruption in the idea of myself.
The 'o' in woman is falling away,
the full cup, the brimming bowl.
I mourn the previous girl. That's how it works:
Each loss triggers the one before it.
I fill my own ghost position,
holding on to a painting sunlight has faded.

*

– *When you have a baby of your own.*
There was no 'if'.
I rode the undeclared out of town,
swinging my lasso after fata morganas,
the road turning to vapour,
quivering
with the impossible ways of being if,
following a broad limestone karst up to wind and sea,
a meadow cut from the depths of a forest,
with an apple-tree as spread as an oak
and a trampoline to bounce on at fifty-eight,
my signature written on the barn roof.

*

I've come to the mouth of blood,
the other end of source.
The ovaries' signal,
the rust-brown residue
of a wine with great legs.
I will let in mid-winter light
one last time:
hello closing parenthesis.

*

I lie anteflexed on the beach
my fat belly, bare deflated breasts,
tanning, wrinkling splendidly,
bikini bottoms electric blue,
eyeshadow Sid Vicious yellow,
lipstick greater than the sum,
water pistols at my hips.
I'll make myself run in, scatter
the water, come out like a candle.

*

Today I see it is a melting,
a softening materialisation,

relieved of fruitfulness.
The lining has become the garment.

*

I'll soon get the hang of changing gear,
  when to break,
        trust the freewheel.
It says Private but no sign of dogs.
        I'll take the underused lane,
        a cure of red clover and poppies,
        seed-tips furring in the sun.

Do things always end when they're fully understood?

The embarrassing hot rain has stopped.
   Celebration carhorns hoot in different tones,
        for ten or fifteen minutes,
            the way a quick tap of joy
                on someone's arm sparks union.

And I remember the startle of dew
this morning,
          how long it lasted,
          how its wide teeming
accomplished the immediate world,
my bare feet,
their grass prints,
and the tuck tuck tuck of the woodpecker,
          cracking for life,
dread and desire polishing its territory's air.

*

What's that sound in the passage?
The jade and coral girdle chimes.

Fair Head

I'd wanted to show our sea could be aquamarine, a proof of Pacific,
given the right light. We'd walked fast towards the headland,
levelled with a family, three young children, ruddy and blonde
in hand-knit sweaters. We overtook them. The kids kept up.
You joked with them, familiar as apple pie and they circled you
pup-like, sniffing, glancing back at their parents, then tumbling forward
bouncing into heather, over streams, blown as bog cotton.
The sky was blameless blue, the gorse sending out its almond signal.
You sparked a race, unspoken, sudden and we were all running
up to the sky, like the first airplane-makers, attempting take-off.
Arms out, you veered left then right, your body blooming with an all-
involving love, a captain with a crew, then the kids, giddy
with strangeness, led up the smooth golden-green to the cliff –
a 200-metre drop none of you could sense.
The edge rose too quick, my stomach tilted through a cabin window.
I yelled 'stop'. I gave chase, snatched the kids by their sleeves,
looked up into the back of time, a tremulous disaster banking on the air.
The parents were far-off, brown strokes in the green.

In the Same Sphere

All afternoon you've been underwater
breathing an allotted amount of air
like a lifespan within a life.

When I went for a walk, the earth took me
solidly, separately on its surface,
an outcrop in gravity's line.

You were everywhere the sea touched,
enormous, cut from our co-existence,
and I, short of breath, from too much sky.

Billedforklaringer

Where the empty rooms are filled with empty rooms
and heads have rolled into wicker baskets to make
such silent space; where the silhouetted cowboy is
a) riding this way, lonesome, b) in a trio of seekers,
or c) pleasantly single, riding into vast vermilion;
where Greenland in watercolours of rain and rock,
is caught on the hop over a valley stream, dated
to help us be there, the history of plank its own device,
contours trying to place the human in this scheme
of green, the head colour; where a 'Tintin in Tibet'
stupa suggests a new sky and polka dots
are punched through the image so we don't forget
what's illusory about this struggle to find shelter
at the northernmost point. He's a liking for clefts
– this is where the woman is –
the lightest geology of chalk on a blackboard as if
there can be no lecture, only looking, *follow this blue,*
and isn't that it, the strength to do the heart justice,
a lump of clay shaken by the hand, skin on the floor
in an unstretched canvas, beyond the concepts,
beyond what we're told colour stands for?

Billedforklaringer ('Picture Explanations') is a book by Danish artist Per Kirkeby, who had a major retrospective at Tate Modern in 2009.

Interior Design

We expected the block of flats across the street
to come down in a wrecking ball, smashing
the spectacle of sky into the small rooms,
the walkways, the lift shafts. Instead it emptied
slowly, fewer lights, loaded skips,
windows boarded up in quiet contagion.
Then there was a hoarding and a mechanical
claw pulling off the outer wall, grinding
through the daylight until the bedrooms
opened out their inside walls of pink, lime,
blue, red, lemon, orange – so disparate,
so chosen, their soft grid glowed, offering
design the building had refused before.
In this tender interim, we began to disagree,
critical as wind. You held back touch.
I hung around, shouting to myself, taking
photos of the metal rods mangled in the breach.
Our gestures reasonable, we listened to the
language of bulldozers and felt above it.
Cement dust gathered on the roofs of cars,
sifted under our door, chalked our lips.
We swept and swept the silent increments.
Outside the ground was cleared.

Il Deserto Rosso

Red gantries stalk the Ravenna docks
a sea architecture to deliver dreams.

Do you see her trying to escape?
'Do you take passengers?'

Hanjin juggernauts emerge from fog.
Edge to edge their iron bodies line
rough decks in washed sienna, each ship
a building afloat with crates that should sink it.

She could have climbed in different shoes.

Great arcing claws rush their bent r's in and out
of the earth, its grass and trees turned white.
Everything on land is solid with disappointment,
a language that burns and moves.
It exhales noisily. Like something criminal she has done.

She pays a worker for his sandwich, eats as if she's homeless.

The factory hums, the streets are empty.
Smoke makes itself a black sky. The management are calm,
civilly dressed. She runs from the end of the pier,
a fast road through water, her green coat living.

To be this dislodged. Not even love or sex can pin her down.
Though some find it appealing in the beach hut,
try to take her wharfside. It seldom helps.

That was the director's best decision.
To leave her helpless.

Vena Cava

Closest to skeleton I've ever been,
hung on a hanger, a lamina I couldn't look at,
a wire-contracted throat
lucidity could not deter, even reciting
give us this day our daily…
but nothing of food's trespass, as if all matter
was poisoned earth
or I was poison.

I looked for the edge of sky,
running into I know not what, stroking
the restless leverets of halved sleep.
Three months of shutting out the moon,
anything that we take to be whole,
with you, my troubled centre, most irrelevant
to the element of fire.

There's such soft-water modesty in betrayal,
slow lipstick, breakdown eyes gripping the ice rail.
Then indignation – hot and wet as platinum.
Wait for it: Oh me, oh my. Oh mine.
To say 'we', the family function,
where belonging is as bread and how we like it.

Mistakes blow on the line.
I haul them damp in my arms.
There will be a mark on the neck
from practice. An accord like music.
Then how to say it is not my ear that hears this?
Even the element of air cannot hold its playing.
I will be as air to music.
The next time. I will record nothing. Download nothing.

Every night I'll rinse until I'm the blue-white
of a fresh eye.
I'll go where my terror thickens: beyond outer
space and beneath anatomy to learn
the fable of the trick of trust,

the what's become of you, the wound that cannot be wounded.
Just wait.
In my sleep, I'll follow used blood back to the heart,
these letters that line up an exit without dying.

Territory

Bloodrush that makes
mountains walk
the cunt's atlas
wettening

Cragged pushy nipple
hand a cup
that drinks its first
each time

Soft white hill
sandbreast birdfoot
tracking from one to the other
to be fair

Melt that was pelvis
thighs rowing rapids
to a shore to just reach
and reach again

Eyes bring themselves open
volition washing
the sockets' nerve
releasing face from skin

How did we once
do this
to one another
without thinking?

Jumpcut

It was an ordinary memory.
Like the others. It kept itself
to itself. Tidy, if you can say
that about how we store things.
In rows. Or bundles. Or labelled crates.
Anyway, like the others, it asked
for nothing, didn't push itself to the front,
was just something we happened to do
on a hot day that took the grass, the sky,
our skin, by surprise. A happy memory:
the lolling about, taking off layers, sun-
creaming each other, sipping from books,
wearing hats, laughing behind sunglasses,
at the end of the garden in late April.
So why, as I sit on a park bench,
rolling up my sleeves, laying my feet
on top of my sandals like small white
loaves, does it come, does it insist
like a film I can't walk out of, on dazzling
me with its rude health, its insouciant beauty,
and why, if it's so ordinary, so happy,
so tidy, am I crying, tears running
from under my sunglasses, some
caught on the rim as they jump.

Kenmare Bay, off Dog Point

Three hours on the black water,
grey cladding Tooth Mountain,
the sky giving the sea a dark skin
of plastic sheeting, creased and creasing,
rocking us up then shrinking,
thudding the hull into hollows
that test the miracle of floating.
We've mere aitches of wood, a bundle
of orange twine, a hook, a feather and
a small lead torpedo. Toasted teacake
jellyfish moither by to a sub-sonic beat.

Then a poke and my line tenses
and a flickering runs up it and the hook
is loaded and I reel in, sensing the fish pound
everything it's ever fought for into this.
'It's big, Hilde,' I shout as if I'm birthing it,
fizzy with surge, and it buckles its cream
and tawny bareness like a young,
sun-tanned limb. Standing to haul,
I'm pinioned by sea-legs of good fortune
and land it, half a metre of shining shock.
I flounce with achievement, property.

Hilde reaches for a stub of wood.
It takes three bashes. Its underwired
mouth is sprung with air. She holds it up.
'Fantastic! Was all worth it.'
I bristle with ethics, try to bathe in mastery.
I have knifed private colour
from the flesh of water.
Yet my arms are proud. I'm sexed
with original drive and the species' win
against the sullen sea. And Hilde, 74,
is beaming – the widowed sailor's rehab.

His Majesty

(for Alizan at Seafield)

Because I imagine a five-bar gate, I agree to carrots
and a five-year-old boy;

because in the city the only horses I see
are mounted by policemen;

because the horse climbs the bank of grass without thinking;

because of immediate muscle, circling breath
and the prehistoric hooves;

because the boy knows to flatten his palm as he balances
each carrot for the fast muzzle;

because, as we walk on, the glad boy is still floating
his small hand under that mobile mouth;

because he laughs when the horse nips his fingertips for more;

because he has enchanted the horse, fearlessness a kind of ripple
his young body has yet to question –

I never once say 'careful', letting everything in.

To Be Found

It's precious, that time that leads up to the finding – Jay Merill

I could go in naked but I won't.
Better to be rescued in a navy swimsuit
looking athletic than be taken for some naturist
who doesn't know the tides; or to be found
washed up, somewhat clothed, less of a shock
to the finder, the blue ballooned limbs enough.
In January, one dark afternoon, I studied
the Thames at the kink of Greenwich, the wasted
docks, the rusting keels, the graceless, prodded
dome, and thought of walking down the stone
steps and in, fully dressed, to swim and keep
swimming away from my cracked, precious
vase of a life. I wanted the effort of sleeving
into the deep, seawards, my mouth jutting,
desperate, at first, not to swallow this bad truth,
then drinking till the filth outside matched that
within, the silt, the turds, the effluent, until I could
rest coated in the water's drag. But today the bay
is quiet and beautiful. June sunlight is smashing
the mirror of the sea into a million pieces of itself.
For three hours I've watched the tide coming in.
This grief will not take me out.

Test, Orange

I am peeling a large, thick-skinned orange.
The rind gives easily as an eyelid. It is the wettest
orange ever opened. I thumb under the peel
and the segments break, flesh staying with skin.
I maul it, juice flooding my fingers, face. I want
the mess gone, the evidence of clumsy process.
Isn't the method of breaking something open important?
There is no kind time for unkind acts but surely a soft
breath can be taken before speech shatters all about it,
a last touch to qualify love's fine and final etiquette.
Then make it quick. You want the bite of blood,
the thick emetic swallow and to hide your mouth
against the cold, the sudden hollow. The way we first
apprise the fruit, carries its eventual breaking down –
the shy night body vanishing, the fireworks or the pulpy
blows of rage. Tufts of orange cling to my nails.
The water will run orange. The throat will be an orange hole,
flamed with nobler endings. I rinse the cloth, my hands.
In our bed, my tested love, we found the will
to torture, proved abominable enough.